# Conte

*This prayer guide could not have been accomplished without the hours of research by Bill Richardson, editing by Sarah Rodden and design by Tina Tomes. They are part of our wonderful SEAPC team. Thank you!*

# Introduction

Where have the children gone? There is a crisis in families and young minds throughout the world. Young people are walking away from the faith of their parents and church. A recent study of some college campuses showed that 59 percent of Christian college students no longer describe themselves as "born again." Why is this happening?

The year was 1882 and the famous philosopher, Friedrich Nietzsche proclaimed that, "God is dead. God remains dead. And we have killed him." This sent shockwaves within the world of higher education and changed the way that the God would be viewed in education. He also said, "Put down the Bible and read Manu." Manu? Who is or what is Manu? In Hindu mythology, it is taught that the gods (with a small "g") created Manu, the first man, who gave life to all humans. Manu wrote a code of conduct called the Manu Smirti. This code helped to set the code of life for followers of Hinduism. This code was used by the colonial government during the British rule of India in 1794 to formulate the Hindu law. These Hindu teachings have worked their way into the world of higher education in the form of conduct, values, and world view. This guide will help you to understand how to pray and intercede for your son or daughter as they enter the world of higher education, and the teaching of these false truths that are being presented as truth. In the words of Manu, "Depend not on another, rather lean upon thyself; trust to thine own exertions: Subjection to another's will gives pain; True happiness consists in self-reliance."

In response to a request from a devoted Christian father concerning his son who has returned from a major university declaring that he no longer believes in Jesus as his Lord and Savior and actually has become an agnostic, we have set forth to equip parents, students and Christian ministries with a 30-day prayer guide to open the eyes of our understanding and to, through loving prayer, non-confrontation, and patient apologetics protect our greatest treasure and investment from a similar fate.

The prayer guide is based on the premise that education is the learning of the words, emotions, actions, disciplines, behaviors, and habits which form culture. To attain a bachelor's degree the student must learn the vocabulary of general thought and a specific discipline. To earn a master's degree, the student must be able to prepare a thesis or presentation of the culture of that discipline including the emotions, actions, behaviors, and habits of the discipline. To earn a doctorate degree, the student must identify a problem in the discipline and solve the problem by creating the words, actions, behaviors, and disciplines necessary to forge a solution.

This process takes the student on a 4-12 year journey in the world of words. Some of the new words contradict or challenge previous thoughts, emotions, actions, behaviors, disciplines, and habits. Bible reading, daily prayer, Christian fellowship, worship, and devotion may give way to study groups, meditation and yoga, exploration of new relationships, exaltation of those who have mastered the new vocabulary, and other new habits that accelerate the mind to a newfound openness. Since family and pastors are of the former culture, they are often left behind in this time of transition. The student has adapted to the campus culture and left behind the culture of their youth.

What is campus culture? It is the commonly accepted habits developed from the new thoughts, emotions, words, actions, behaviors, and habits of those in the new surroundings which become a life stance for the future development of the student. The key people they meet will become those with whom they interact for the duration of their career. New relationships replace those of the former culture and with each relationship come thoughts, emotions, words, actions, behaviors, and habits.

How then does the loving Christian parent maintain a voice for Christ through this transition? It all begins with prayer. There is no act more loving than to set aside your hurt and fear and come to the Lord on behalf of your child. In the next thirty days we are going to teach you a basic vocabulary of the thoughts and words of the new agnostic culture, and each day we will give Bible verses to pray over and to prepare your loving, non-confrontational, and patient apologetic. By praying through this booklet each month, you will become equipped so when your child expresses the thoughts and words of the new culture, you will have a Bible-based response and your heart will be tuned through prayer to reassure your child of your love and the love Jesus has for them.

Be prepared, they are going to come to you. They may try to shock you a bit, but stay steady on the word of God and respond with patient love and clear understanding. The guide is designed to help you prayerfully understand four aspects of your child's educational journey: Campus Culture, Choices, Philosophy, and Humanism. We have chosen these 4 areas as the result of years of study and interviews with current professors at major universities across America. While there are generalities in the statements, the words you will learn are in daily use both in liberal arts schools and within the scientific disciplines. These are the words that attempt to replace the word of God in your child's life.

At the back of this book, you will find a glossary of philosophical terms, a list of the most influential modern philosophers, and a selection of philosophical quotes. We hope that you will find these resources to be helpful in understanding what your student is learning, and that they will serve as a starting point for meaningful discussion with your student.

Let us believe together that your child will be equipped and will stand for the Savior who loves them and has given His life for them.

# Campus Culture

# Campus Culture

Christians are hypocrites... Right?

"There have been a lot of monster Christians ... Hitler was a Christian."
Whoopi Goldberg*

Do an internet search for the words "Christians are" and you will get a sad picture of what the world thinks of Christians. The top results for this search are: "Christians are hypocrites," "Christians are narrow-minded," "Christians are evil," "Christians are idiots," "Christians are terrorists and they are all crazy." Many people have a negative reaction against Christianity and Christians because they don't understand what it is to be a Christian, because of past hurts, moral failures, or being forced to go to Church as a child. But on the other hand, many people just don't get Christianity. In other words, they really don't have a strong understanding of what Christianity actually is.

Summit Ministries published a piece entitled "Why Students Don't 'Get It'" on this very topic, where they ask: "How is it that students who are so deeply engrossed in church culture and who have more access to the Bible, Christian literature, youth programs, and other resources than any generation that has lived since the founding of the church, can be so confused about what Christianity actually is and why it matters? How is it that they possess such a truncated, neutered view of the Kingdom? How is it that these students just don't 'get it?'"

The disconnect between true Christianity and what teens believe is dramatically revealed in a recent book titled *Soul Searching: The Religious and Spiritual Lives of American Teenagers*, written primarily by Christian Smith, a University of North Carolina sociologist. Smith and his colleagues conducted the largest survey to date of religious beliefs among teenagers. Based on these extensive interviews, Smith writes that many students who claim to be Christians believe a host of ideas that are not anything close to orthodox Christianity. What they actually believe is something Smith identifies as "moralistic therapeutic deism." On this view, the only point of faith is to be good, to feel good, and to have a God to always call on for help without expecting anything in return. This is a far cry from a biblical view of God and our relationship to Him."**

**"By this all men will know that you are My disciples, if you have love for one another." John 13:35**

*http://thefederalist.com/2015/11/18/whoopi-goldberg-christians-are-just-dangerous-as-muslims-because-hitler/
**Students Abandoning the Faith Why It Happens and What We Can Do, http://www.summit.org/resources essays/students-abandoning-the-faith/ by John Stonestreet and Chuck Edwards

# Day 1

## University and Universalism

All thoughts are given equal opportunity in a Universal environment. The student begins to reflect on their value in the cosmos and impact on karma. They are encouraged to blend with, tolerate, and accept the diversity of personal thoughts, values, and life stances expressed by faculty and classmates. Many of their freshman classes will be held in large lecture halls with hundreds of students where they will not be able to question or challenge the thoughts and values expressed. They are expected to learn the thoughts of the new culture without question or comment.

My student's name is: _____

My prayer time is: _____

My Bible promise is: _____

_____

**"Your word is a lamp for my feet, a light for my path."
Psalm 119:105**

**"God has not given us a spirit of fear; but of power, love, and a sound mind." 2 Timothy 1:7**

**"Jesus said, 'I am the way, the truth, and the life, no man comes to the Father but by me.'" John 14:7**

 *Father, in the name of Jesus, I ask you to watch over my child. Guard their mind from the new words and thoughts they are hearing and seeing at school. Put angels around them to keep them in the right path.*

# Day 2

## *Words*

Words convey thought and compel to action. People live in words. The most important word you will say to your student during this transition is the word that follows, "You are ..."

Your child will receive your assessment and live in it. The word you speak will become the protector or the justifier in the next four years of your child's life. Words create emotion. They are the rock that is thrown in the still pond that stirs the water.

Your child is going to be inundated with words. They are going to hear words, learn words, and write new words. Some of the words they will hear will be words that you forbade in their childhood and hopefully did not use. Other words are going to describe chemistry, poetry, physics, and math. Some of the words are going to be from Plato and Socrates while others are going to be from Sartre and Nietzsche. Many of the words they learn will be ancient words filled with beauty and meaning and others will be wasted words of frustrated failures. But they are in a word factory for sure and to gain their degree, they are going to have to learn thousands of new words, each of which will be conveying new thoughts and compel to new behaviors. (A glossary of the 100 most used terms is included for you in the back of this book.)

They will take the basic psychology courses and analyze why you are the way you are, and how you made them to be who they are, and how they feel about you and how you did that. Enjoy that ride and do not defend yourself for in their fourth year they will learn that they are an individual and you and God really didn't have anything to do with that.

When they register for courses, go online and find out what books they will read. From Amazon you can get used ones cheap. Just read the glossary and you will know the words your child will be feeding you at Thanksgiving, and Christmas, and hopefully Spring Break.

My student's first word was: _____

My student's favorite book was: _____

My student made a commitment to Christ on: _____

My student's first prayer was: _____


**"In the Beginning was the Word and the Word was with God and the Word was God." John 1:1**

**"How can a young person stay on the path of purity? By living according to your word." Psalm 119:9**

**"Therefore get rid of all moral filth and the evil that is so prevalent and humbly accept the Word planted in you, which can save you." James 1:21**

 *Father, in the name of Jesus I ask you to help me to enjoy these years with my child. I am a bit nervous about their going off to school, and the things to which they will be exposed. Help me to make the time more successful by speaking the right words — your words — to them. Bless them, I pray.*

# Day 3

## *Actions*

While most schools make an attempt at proper decorum, the first few weeks away from home and making new friends are a very precarious time for new students. Fraternities and sororities make their pitch to the young person with promises of future favor and an elite level while at the university. Peer groups begin to form around dorm assignments and class schedules. Clubs form around schools of thought or particular talents.

Your student is going to find a place to fit in, often looking for a more accepting life stance than their home life. They often want to stretch their wings and fly. Our phrase has been, "If you want to soar with the eagles, you cannot walk with the turkeys."

Your student may try different actions, standards of dress and appearance, language use, or relationships that were not a part of their upbringing. You will begin to observe a change in them through this testing period. Once does not a habit make, except with some drugs. Do not be overbearing, but rather gently reaffirm your love and your standards.

You may observe the "shame game" in which your student acts as though they have done some horrible thing and pull away from you with anger or shame. This is a time to express your love. Love conquers fear and while you do not condone the actions, you must gently remove the shame.

**"There is no fear in love. But perfect love drives out fear."
1 John 4:18**

**"Love is patient. love is kind. [...] it is not easily angered, it keeps no record of wrong." 1 Corinthians 13:4-5**

The last time I told my student "I love you" was: _____

My favorite way to express love for my student is: _____

My monthly student care package will include: _____

_____

My student's favorite meal is: _____

**"Brothers and Sisters, If someone is caught in a sin, you who live by the Spirit should seek to restore that person gently." Galatians 6:1**

 *Father, please help me to love through the shame and maintain and restore an open and loving relationship with my child. I refuse to condemn them with my words, but ask you to break through in their life. Give me the peace and calm to not react angrily, but to seek to restore. I bring my pain to you.*

# Day 4

## *Emotions*

Separation from family and culture norms gives rise to a myriad of emotions. Your student wants to be accepted in the campus culture. They will be attracted to a father replacement, a sympathetic male, and a nurturing female. Looking for emotional stability, they will form relationships. These relationships will form their life stance for their future. You can no longer control their actions. Prayer is the means by which you can ask the Lord to watch over them, bring the right people to them, and protect them from every device of the enemy.

Acceptance in new groups, discovery of new attractions, and a sense of success and failure cause the student to have brief experiences of intense mental activity and a high level of pleasure and displeasure. Any Saturday in the fall you can watch this phenomenon occur by tuning in to a college football game. Emotions rise and fall and the champion is crowned. Hugs are given, faces are painted, and chests are bared as the student section identifies with the perceived emotion of the players. What they do not know is that the player is being trained to focus that emotion as a driving force to achieve goals and the student section frenzy has little to do with the players' performance until victory is won. Then, the party is on.

Governing emotion is a sign of maturity. Maintaining poise no matter what the grade or social standing is one of the life lessons we hope the student learns at the university. 19%* of this year's freshmen will obtain their bachelor's degree in 4 years. They are the ones who have mastered emotion.

**"We have this hope as an anchor for the soul, firm and secure." Hebrews 6:19**

**"In God I trust and am not afraid. What can man do to me?" Psalm 56:11**

Rom 8:31

My campus student ministry contact is: _____

_____

There is a small Christian group meeting in: _____

_____

I will reassure my student of my love by: _____

**"He was despised and rejected by mankind, a man of
suffering and familiar with pain." Isaiah 53:3**

 *Jesus, you knew the pain of rejection. You were in a different
culture with the contradiction of sinners, yet you did not sin.
Please give my child the ability to draw strength from you to
withstand the emotions of change. Help them to keep their focus.*

Don - norestrictions (except driving)
Duane - Lee's brother

*19% of students at public universities graduate in 4 years. (NY Times)

14

10/18/22

# Day 5

## *Behaviors*

The campus culture challenges new students to adapt their behaviors to new cultural norms. Justification of a separation from the previous Christian standards is the peer pressure we hope our children can resist. It is very difficult to stand for the old culture when the new is in your face. We look to campus ministries, churches, administrations, and faculty to curb the excesses of campus culture, but the life your child will live will be their choice.

Enticement is on every side. Acceptance is the key word here. If a pledge adapts their behavior, they are accepted into the fraternity or sorority. If language is adapted to a group, then the individual is accepted in the group. When everyone is doing it, it is very hard to say, "I am not everyone, I am someone."

Parents hope that they have ingrained in the child a sense of proper and improper behavior. Hopefully they have lived their values so the 18 years they have spent with this child will not be able to be eroded in the four years of campus life. There are some statistics that say it doesn't make a bit of difference if the child went to a Christian high school, a public high school, or was home-schooled; the percentages of separation from Christian culture remain the same. The faith of their fathers must become their own.

You have sown incorruptible seed in the heart of your child. Your child has memorized the word, sung the word, read the word, and heard the word. Speak to that word. Call forth fruit of the incorruptible seed in your child's life and remind them that they were once of the world, but have been born again.

**"Train up a child in the way he should go, and when he is old he will not depart from it." Proverbs 22:6**

My student made a public profession of faith on: _____

My student has shown good faith in the past through: _____

_____

I will reinforce acceptance by: _____

_____

**"For you have been born again, not of corruptible seed, but by the word of God which lives and abides forever."**
**1 Peter 1:23**

**"I have hidden your word in my heart, that I might not sin against you." Psalm 119:11**

*Father, in the name of Jesus I speak to the word that is in the heart of my child. You bring forth fruit of righteousness. You watch over the word to perform it. Father, cause fruit to come forth in this child. Cause them to take a stand in your name and hunger and thirst for righteousness.*

# Day 6

## *Habits*

Habits are behaviors that are accepted by the majority of a culture and are repeated without thought. Actions need justification. There has to be a moral, ethical question answered before an action is taken. Behaviors have settled the thought process and the individual no longer has to answer the moral or ethical question because one answer fits all situations. For example; if I accept the thought that there is no supreme being that will dispatch consequence for my behavior, and that the school or police do not have the right to govern my words and behaviors, then I have become a free moral agent and do not have to answer for my behaviors. It is just me, and you will have to deal with it — this is who I am.

Study habits are a precursor to attaining a degree. They are a set of behaviors that have been ingrained in the student by a parent or teacher who saw potential in the child and gave the time and care to establish those habits that would see the child through to maturity. Through the process this coaching individual stayed near the student and monitored their success. They were probably the one who wrote a reference letter for the student's college application.

In the campus culture, they are no longer there. The student is to have a faculty advisor, but these are often far removed from the quality of the parent, teacher, or coach. So the student feels very alone and afraid to fail. The prop is gone and cannot be replaced in the new culture. However, Jesus is there. The Holy Spirit is there. And your prayers, notes of encouragement, and video chat time are going to get this child retrenched in the habits you have instilled and cause them to always measure the "why" for every action.

Habits determine schedule. I will talk with my student, hear their schedule, and schedule calls and video chats for _____ (day) at _____ (time).

My scheduled prayer time is: _____

"For I know whom I have believed and am persuaded that He is able to keep that which I have committed unto Him against that day." 2 Timothy 1:12

"And it was so, when the days of their feasting were gone about, that Job sent and sanctified them, and rose up early in the morning, and offered burnt offerings according to the number of them all: for Job said, It may be that my sons have sinned, and cursed God in their hearts. Thus did Job continually." Job 1:5

"though he may stumble, he will not fall, for the Lord upholds him with His hand." Psalm 37:24

*Father, You have many sons and daughters. You know all about the habits of each of them. I lift my child to you. If he has sinned against you, I ask you to forgive him and restore him to paths of righteousness. If he needs to confess the sin, lest it become a habit, I pray that his heart will be turned to mine and that together we may receive your loving forgiveness.*

# Day 7

## *Campus Ministries*

The school that you have selected has several really good campus ministries. We can help you find one that will work in prayer and activities to help your student find the cultural underpinnings with which they have been raised. Campuses are also surrounded by churches. The question is, "How do we make the connection with a ministry or church outreach?"

Using the internet and available websites will give you opportunity to directly contact a pastor or student pastor at a church of your denomination. You can also find information on campus ministries at your university website. But this is just a step for information. Your child will have to respond to the ministry's attempt to contact them. This is where prayer gets very involved and a casual question will help.

Your student is meeting many people. Each of them is going to speak different "words" to them. In the desire to flow with the new culture, your student will respond with actions that will be acceptable to the new friend. Pray with all you have that this friend is a believer in Jesus Christ. Begin to pray daily for righteous relationships. Pray for a dorm life or apartment life in which Christ is exalted and ask very gently about the new people in your student's life.

At the end of this prayer guide you will find the contact information for the national office of recommended campus ministries. They are ready to serve you with information about your school.

The campus ministry activities are posted at: _____

The church nearest to my student is: _____

The pastor's name is: _____

"Forsake not the assembling of yourselves together, as the manner of some is;" Hebrews 10:25

"A man who has friends must himself be friendly, but there is a friend who sticks closer than a brother." Proverbs 18:24

"By this shall all men know that you are my disciples, if you have love one for another." John 13:35

 *Father, in the name of Jesus, I ask you to join my child to a vibrant Christian fellowship. Please make their first friends Christians and bring them to a good solid Bible-believing church or ministry. Let the word in them give them wisdom to choose the right friends and fellowship.*

Choices

# Choices

America is a country that takes great pride in the freedom to choose. Nowhere in America is this freedom celebrated more than on the university campus. Each student enjoys the freedom to plot their own career course, major subject, program of study, class schedule, and professor. Actually the student is given the option of dropping a class if, in the first three meetings, they find that it was not what they expected. The student will make further choices in friends, partner or spouse, stay or transfer, finish or drop, fellowships or fraternities, Jesus or humanism.

When Joshua stood at the gateway to the Promised Land, he realized that each member of the community had choices to make and that the most important would be their faith. He challenged the people, "But if you don't want to worship the Lord, then choose right now! Will you worship the same idols your ancestors did? Or since you are living on land that once belonged to the Amorites, maybe you will worship their gods. I won't. My family and I are going to worship and obey the Lord." (Joshua 24:15)

Your student is living in the bastion of humanism. They are going to be compelled to worship the gods of that land. They are going to have to take a very strong stand in that place. It is not an exaggeration to bring up Joshua, for the student stands at the threshold of his dream.

In sections 3 and 4 of your prayer guide you will learn the gods of this age and how they got to the campus. You will be equipped to respond in a very gentle way to the new words your student will throw at you. It is essential that you cover your child in prayer every day. They may try to be adult, and the world around them may refer to them as adult, but they are not ready for the onslaught of anti-Christ thought that is about to come their way.

It was Karl Marx who quoted the phrase crafted by the Marquis de Sade "religion... is the opiate of the masses." Your student is going to hear in science courses, philosophy courses, and the entire required course packages for all medical arts the mantra of no creation, no God, ancient myths, and they are going to have to make a choice as to what they believe. Marx declared, "Whoever holds the children holds the future." Now is the time of testing for your child. As our dear friend said, "What has happened to my son?"

Together, we can form a prayer shield over your son or daughter; but, as it was with Job, you are going to have to take the daily prayer very seriously and develop it more fully. We are giving you 3 verses each day, but you must search out the Word of God to text or email to your student. In a very gentle and non-confrontational way, you have to reestablish daily your faith in God and in your child to make the right choices. The Lord is faithful and He will answer your prayers and give you wisdom to go with your love.

You are not alone in your desire to see your student excel in this experience. Your child should come forth Christ-centered, Bible-based, and Holy Spirit filled, with excellence in education. The university you have selected will do all in their power to prepare your student to lead in their generation. And praying parents the nation over will join with you to sustain the spiritual life of your most precious treasure.

# Day 8

## *Careers*

In previous generations the question of career was tied to income. The thought was a four year degree will add an extra zero to your annual income. And, today, that thought is expressed in much of the rhetoric concerning further education. But today's student is motivated by another thought. What can I do that will make the most significant impact in the global community?

Will it be education, agriculture, finance, medicine, or psychology? Should I take a career in international business and establish a social enterprise to alleviate the suffering of the masses? Should I pursue a career in international law and attack human trafficking? Should I study abroad to qualify for leadership positions in the multinational corporations or the growing number of NGOs working in the developing world? Should I study veterinary medicine and save endangered species?

Your student has two years of general studies before they declare a major. During this time, encourage them to seek the Lord, and pray about where He would use them to bring His solutions to the needs of man.

My student wants a career in: _____

This desire began when: _____

My student is being counseled by: _____

My student's advisor is: _____

My student's head of department is: _____

"We can make our plans, but the Lord determines our steps." Proverbs 16:9

"Plans fail for lack of counsel, but with many advisers they succeed." Proverbs 15:22

"If any of you lacks wisdom, let him ask God, who gives generously to all without reproach, and it will be given him." James 1:5

*Father, in the name of Jesus I ask you to give us all wisdom concerning the career track of my child. I pray that you will surround him with Godly counsel and that your wisdom will come through them. I pray that he will seek you with every decision and choice set before him. I believe that you will set his feet in the right way.*

# Day 9

## *Majors*

Declaring a major is the directional step in the student's life. Once this choice is made, facility and faculty are assigned by the university to attain the bachelor's and prepare the student for study toward a master's degree. There are required courses and options for the student. Here they have to be careful to fulfill the requirements of their major or they will be in school a fifth or sixth year. Choosing classes is very important here and advice should be sought. Professors in the major subjects are the key to future growth. Many required texts were actually written by the professor or by someone who they really affirm as the best in their field. The student is choosing to whom he will submit himself for the majority of the next two years. His heaviest study load will be determined by these major subjects.

Through the general courses, the student's math and English, writing and conceptual logic have been developed as well as a world view and life stance. He is now ready to build the layer of language that will bridge to the master's program. Approximately one in three of his freshman year classmates have likely either dropped out, failed, or transferred to another school by their sophomore year.* He is in the survivor group and has demonstrated the academic capability to handle these next level courses.

It is good at this point for the student to shadow someone in the coming profession to understand how the courses they are going to take will build them to the career. During Spring Break or the summer, they should consider a short term mission trip to sharpen their world view as they start this preparation. There are unlimited opportunities in the Christian global community for American youth with a bachelor's degree. The student should have opportunity to understand that the Lord is forming them to make that significant impact they desire to make.

Our phrase is, "Finish the degree and come and see me."

* http://colleges.usnews.rankingsandreviews.com/best-colleges/rankings/national-universities/freshmen-least-most-likely-return

The most influential teacher in my student's life was: _____

They can be contacted at: _____

Campus ministries offers short term trips to: _____

SEAPC offers Career Link trips to: _____

(You can learn about career link trips at the end of this book)

**"But you must continue in the things which you have learned and been assured of, knowing from whom you have learned them, and that from childhood you have known the Holy Scriptures, which are able to make you wise for salvation through faith which is in Christ Jesus. All Scripture is given by inspiration of God, and is profitable for doctrine, for reproof, for correction, for instruction in righteousness, that the man of God may be complete, thoroughly equipped for every good work."**
**2 Timothy 3:14-17**

*Father, in the name of Jesus, I ask you to breathe life into the scriptures that my child has learned and to remind him of the quality of the people who taught him. I pray that his mind would be filled with the words that he has learned. I know the word of God is sharp and powerful and I ask that your power be manifest in directing him to the major that will result in your perfect plan for him.*

# Day 10

## *Courses*

The program of study to which your student has submitted is built in layers. In the first two years they are challenged to study and use new words. In high school a book was taught as a part of a unit, taking about a month. Now they accelerate to a book a week. Those who can take this speed have learned to underscore key words and memorize those words so that they begin to be used in papers and discussion.

Each course has its key vocabulary. A theme, or unit of study, is said to "evolve" as one set of words builds upon another. The course then "evolves" over the semester. So thought and actions also evolve as the student replaces former, Christ-based, created thought with evolving self-based choices. This is the process that humanistic education has developed to bring your son or daughter out of the "bondage" of ancient mythological concepts like "God" into a more "enlightened" state of wisdom generating from within the human spirit. If there is no God, then there is no creation, there is no set or arbitrary ethic or morality so everything evolves.

In the university environment this train of thought becomes the denial of the creator and the exaltation of the human spirit. You must listen to your child's course selection, check them online, find the books they are required to read, and prepare yourself with the word of God to call them back to a Christ-centered world view. This is the battleground for the faith of your child.

My student's courses this term are: _____

_____

_____

The instructors are: _____

"For the weapons of our warfare are not carnal but mighty in God for pulling down strongholds, casting down arguments and every high thing that exalts itself against the knowledge of God, bringing every thought into captivity to the obedience of Christ," 2 Corinthians 10:4-5

"I do not cease to give thanks for you, making mention of you in my prayers: that the God of our Lord Jesus Christ, the Father of glory, may give to you the spirit of wisdom and revelation in the knowledge of Him, the eyes of your understanding being enlightened; that you may know what is the hope of His calling, what are the riches of the glory of His inheritance in the saints, and what is the exceeding greatness of His power toward us who believe, according to the working of His mighty power which He worked in Christ when He raised Him from the dead […]" Ephesians 1: 16-20

"I am reminded of your sincere faith which first lived in your grandmother Lois and in your mother Eunice and, I am persuaded, now lives in you also." 2 Timothy 1:5

*Heavenly Father, I believe you are the only true God, the Creator of the Universe and that through your Son, our Lord Jesus Christ, you made all things and sustain them. My child is being taught that you are no longer and you are not real. This argument against you is being fed to him on a daily basis. With your mighty power, I bring these thoughts captive. I pull down these thoughts and I ask you to enlighten his understanding and stir up the faith that is in him. I trust you, for you are the Father of all who call upon your name.*

11-8-22

# Day 11

## *Friends*

Trust, when lost, takes years to regain. Broken promises, separations, and divorce have left a deep wound on this generation. Self-determination and moral intelligence are rushing to fill the void. Those who said they did not want to force faith on their children have generally not demonstrated trustworthy family standards or ethics, either. Commitments made in our youth change as do we, just as our word of 10 years ago may change as situations change. Because of this lack of family standards, the student then forms intense friendships.

There is a reason why the sitcom "Friends" is one of the most watched in entertainment history, just as there is a reason the people we meet on Facebook ask to be "friended." In the first week on campus, the student makes many new friends. Each one comes with a story of love. Either missing love, or fulfilled love, but a story of love. This gives rise to the first fraternity party, the first study date, the first close roommate, the first of many friendships. Some will last, and some will not, but each will make a mark on the searching soul of the student.

The good news is we have a friend who is closer than a brother. We have a friend who will give his life, not take ours. We have a friend who will not use us or abuse us, who does not play the emotional ride of moral intelligence, but will meet us where we are and love us with unconditional love.

My student's new friends are: _____

My trust building program includes asking questions and listening closely. My time to listen is: _____

"Greater love has no man than this, that a man lay down his life for his friends." John 15:13

"A man who has friends must show himself friendly, But there is a friend who sticks closer than a brother." Proverbs 18:24

"I no longer call you servants, because a servant does not know his master's business. Instead, I have called you friends, for everything that I learned from my Father I have made known to you." John 15:15

 *Lord, please forgive me for the violation of trust with my child. Please surround him with your presence and let him know your love in a very personal way. Give him discernment to know who his true friends are. Protect him from being used and abused. Lord, be the friend that is closer than a brother.*

# Day 12

## *Time Management*

How the environment has changed. No one to wake you up and send you off to school with a good breakfast. No one to be sure you are in at night and resting well. No one to pick you up after school and listen to the day's events. Thank God for smart phones and video chatting.

Making the transition from a book a semester or year to a book a week is a very demanding change for any student, and the one without sound study habits and the understanding that education is words is not going to survive the first year at a university. The student is expected to learn a minimum of 10 new words or concepts in every chapter or each week. Many of the better high school students register for too many credits in their first term. Wanting to get off to a fast start, they bury themselves in too many new words and concepts and find that it is no longer easy to attain a good grade.

Managing the perfect attendance necessary to keep the pace and the demand of out of the classroom time to be prepared for the class is more than 41% of students can handle.* And the social aspects of the university, new culture, new friends, and new life patterns are waiting to rush in to any spaces in schedule and personal discipline. This is when Bible study, prayer, worship, and Christian fellowship known in the old culture crumble.

The student who works a part-time job to have the finances for school is in an even more difficult time of it. Being realistic in scheduling is essential. Help is best found through a campus ministry. There are many wonderful approved on-campus ministries to speak into this time management need.

The demands upon my student's time are: _____

_____

_____

I can help by: _____

_____

I will reinforce Bible words through: _____

"Teach us to number our days, that we may gain a heart of wisdom." Psalm 90:12

"Therefore do not worry about tomorrow, for tomorrow will worry about its own things. Sufficient for the day is its own trouble." Matthew 6:34

"Do you not say, 'There are still four months and then comes the harvest'?" John 4:35

*Dear Lord, please help my child to be focused on the purpose of being in school. Help him to schedule wisely and find good Christian counsel to help him make his decisions. As the demands increase, help him to understand the terms used in his courses. Let him grasp the vocabulary quickly. Help him to manage his time and not put off to the end of the term the papers and study needed to succeed.*

Trinity – cancer
Frank – lung cancer
Chris – chemo
Sue & Joel trip to CA, rides
Julie's son Stephan
Sue's brother – Dwayne
Jim Shuman – Tx for bipolar
Kayla – baby premie
Barbara's – daughter, Steven

*41% of college students will not complete their degrees within 6 years (US Department of Education).

Christmas Eve 6:30 Lifegate

# Day 13

## *Self-Worth*

Here is a crisis point among many students. The Valedictorian of last year's high school graduating class is now just another face in a thousand freshmen. All the accolades mean nothing in this new culture. Like the fading newspaper clippings and the faded roses, the self-esteem of the super producer begins to wane. At this point the student needs some encouragement from home, not about who they have been, but who they will become. They need encouragement for the new group is very highly competitive and will use your child for gain in their own quest for identity.

Face time becomes so very important. Get a phone with a video chatting app and familiarize yourself with using it. A face to face encouragement and a daily text of encouragement will carry the student through this time. The new culture is not going to validate your child by their past accomplishments.

As a Christian parent, you understand that this child is a particular child of promise and you have a promise for their lives. Now is the time to remind them of those promises and your confidence in them and in the Lord to validate them.

My video chat appointment is _____ at _____ .

I will support my student's self-worth through: _____

_____

I will approach our pastor, youth pastor, or _____ to encourage my student.

"For He made Him who knew no sin to be sin for us, that
we might become the righteousness of God in Him."
2 Corinthians 5:21

"And the Lord will make you the head and not the
tail; you shall be above only, and not be beneath [...]"
Deuteronomy 28:13

*Heavenly Father, please quicken to our child the fact that they are
a special gift from you. They were sent here to earth through their
natural parents for specific purpose at this time. They are above
and not beneath the factors of this life. They are the head and not
the tail. Please make their unique purpose real to them.*

# Day 14

## *Christian Fellowship*

Sunday worship is one of many opportunities your student will have to grow in Christian fellowship. The campus ministries live to get Christian students together. These are great places to make new friends, find out sound advice, get academic help, and just relax and have a good time. The campus ministries range from local church outreaches to global fellowships. Your student should be gently encouraged to find fellowship there.

Many campuses are experiencing great growth in their ministries. There is an emphasis on prayer, worship, and the study of the word of God that speaks to a coming youth movement that will eclipse any the church has known before. There is no reason why your student should not become a part of this wave of the Spirit of God

**"Not forsaking the assembling of ourselves together, as the manner of some is;" Hebrews 10:25**

**"They were continually devoting themselves to the apostles' teaching and to fellowship […]" Acts 2:42**

**"But if we walk in the light, as he is in the light, we have fellowship with one another, and the blood of Jesus his Son cleanses us from all sin." 1 John 1:7**

 *Father, in the name of Jesus I come to you to ask you to draw my child into fellowship with other Christians on her campus. Holy Spirit, you know who is good for her and who is not. I ask you to bring her together with believers with whom she can grow in you.*

# Philosophy

# Philosophy

"[…] A little philosophy inclineth man's mind to atheism;" - Sir Francis Bacon

The word "philosophy" is made up of two Greek roots, "philo" meaning "love," and "sophia" meaning "wisdom." According to Richard Jewell, in his text Experiencing the Humanities, in a general sense, philosophy is the love of wisdom or to be more specific, "the pursuit, study of, and enquiry into wisdom."* According to Jewell, some of the greatest philosophers have called philosophy the "art of thinking," while others have viewed it as the "systematic study of human thought and feeling." Finally, Jewell notes that some have said of philosophy that, "in real life people think about things, in philosophy they think about thinking." However, as we read in Proverbs 9:10, "The fear of the LORD is the beginning of wisdom, And the knowledge of the Holy One is understanding." (NASB)
Common sense

As we delve into philosophy and philosophers, we will need to start thinking about how the world and Christians are different when they think and how our thinking is affected by the educational systems, the cultures, and religions of the world. This section of this guide will be the start of our journey in "thinking about thinking," as Jewell puts it. Jewell also notes that most philosophers like to think about their feelings, and analyze the various types of feelings whether artistic or emotional feelings, or even intuitions. In fact, there is one more step to take: one simply can call all thoughts and all feelings "perceptions." Usually the word "perception" means the ability to see, hear, or become aware of something through one's senses in the fleshly world versus the heavenly world. The difference is world views. As Christians and believers we are called to have a Christian world view and to see how everything in our lives is ordained by God, and that everything in life is not just a set of random events and experiences for us to think about.

In this section we are going to mention the thinkers that formed the pathway to humanism and away from God. They range from the 17th to the 20th century and it is their words that your student will have to learn to pass the required philosophy courses. Most schools dedicate six credits or 90 hours of instruction to this area of study. The first 45 hours are to acquaint the student with general philosophical thought and vocabulary. It is often an online course or one of those large classes of 200 or more. Its purpose is to introduce the student to the thoughts and initial vocabulary they will find as they continue their course of study, no matter what major they declare.

The second 45 class hours will come in their senior year as they learn to apply the vocabulary to the discipline into which they have now devoted 110 credit hours or three and a half years of study. This level of philosophy is taught in a smaller classroom setting with 20-30 students. The student is expected to converse and write using the new words to express thought.

In your communication with the freshman, as they understand that the writers are saying that there is either no God or nature is god, or we all together make god, or god is the extension of our fears, you will need to gently refer to the actions of God in your life, and what Jesus has done for you. They are being told that miracles do not happen, that there is no external spiritual power that intervenes in the lives of men, and that intelligent people do not believe the Bible or the stories of the Bible.

When you see that your student is registered for Philosophy 101, get ready to gently share with them the small things that happen in your life, and have happened in theirs so that their faith is living and their relationship with Jesus is sustained. At some point they may say some pretty hurtful things as they are trying the arguments that are being fed them. Take a deep breath and respond with simple, true, unexaggerated testimonies from their life.

One very powerful remembrance to share with them is your prayers for them as a child, that they are a very special and unique gift from God, and that they are not an accident of nature, but a very special gift who you love and cherish.

Above all do not get drawn into a discussion of the philosopher of the week. He died a long time ago and his words are dead with him. Remember, the person with a testimony is never at the mercy of a person with an argument. Recall the good things of God and pray.

*Experiencing the Humanities, http://www.tc.umn.edu/~jewel001/humanities/book/5philosophy.htm, by Richard Jewell

# Day 15

## *René Descartes*
### *31 March 1596 – 11 Feb. 1650*

*I think, therefore I am*

I cannot help but wonder what René would think about if he had ridden in a car, sat in air-conditioning, seen a television, or had a smartphone. If he had been in a vibrant local church in which people regularly felt the divine presence and saw confirmed miracles, things that cannot be explained away by scientific means. Nonetheless, he is the father of modern philosophy. How thought projected in the seventeenth century can be called "modern" and can be the standard for today amazes me until I understand that it was he who introduced "methodic doubt." Methodic doubt is what changes "What is true" to "Of what can I be certain?"

With this move, Descartes displaced God as the authority on truth, and instead delegated this authority to humanity. This shift in authority became the structure for modernity. The results of this, namely a break from church doctrine and Christianity's truths, and a movement towards people making their "own" laws, can still be seen today.

Indeed, this is the father of doubt. A method of assessing what is in the Bible, taught by pastors, and especially parents by the students understanding of life issues. "Hath God said?" The work of the original doubt caster continues in this father and his offspring. As the student learns methodic doubt and begins to apply it, they turn into a reasoning adult, a subject, and agent as opposed to a child obedient to God.

Get those testimonies of the goodness of the Lord ready. Be prepared to share from your life and the memories of the child how their personal relationship with and faith in Jesus has brought them through. Yes, they have to learn the words of Descartes but they do not have to leave the faith to become an adult. Yes, faith is very simplistic. Yes, we have the faith of a little child. Yes, to the intellectual it is almost laughable, but the lame walk, the blind see, and the nation that serves the Lord prospers.

My student's first personal encounter with God was: _____

My student received Christ on: _____

We shared the Holy presence through: _____

"But as many as received Him, to them He gave the right to become children of God, to those who believe in His name" John 1:12

"And the Word became flesh and dwelt among us, and we beheld His glory, the glory as of the only begotten of the Father, full of grace and truth." John 1:14

"The Spirit Himself bears witness with our spirit that we are children of God." Romans 8:16

*Father, in the name of Jesus who we do believe, I ask you to remind my child of the wonderful things you have done in their life. The Doubter, the Father of lies, is trying to cause doubt and confusion in their mind. Holy Spirit, I ask you to toughen my child in a very special way. Let her feel the embrace of your love and the reality of your presence. Give me the right remembrance to share in Jesus name.*

1st - never accept a thing as true until I knew it as such w/o a single doubt

Glenn Shultz
Johnny - house church
Boldness
Darren + Becky + Child
Miranda came home from MT
Mary - Vacation CA /Mexico

our country/state
county

41

# Day 16

## *Immanuel Kant*
### *22 April, 1724 – 12 Feb 1804*

Kant struggled with the thought that if man replaced God as the moral agent, then what of the metaphysical realm which, in his personal experience, could not be denied. That there is something or someone who is higher than the physical and therefore temporal realm would mean that man could not determine his own moral code or ethic.

This is a theme that repeats through all philosophy. If you take away God, His word, His presence, then where does morality come from? This is the seed that has grown into moral intelligence, the absence of classroom discipline, and today the transgender movement. If I feel like a girl today, then I am a girl for today.

His solution is to say, "It is only real if it is within the grasp of my reason." So today's student comes out a relativist, saying "Well mom, that faith in Jesus is great for you, and I am glad you have it, but it has not fit within the grasp of my reason, therefore for me it is not real."

Key concepts associated with Kant: Reason is the source of morality; Aesthetics (application of external stimuli to affect internal change) arises from a faculty of disinterested judgment; and space and time are forms of our understanding.

Yes, your student has to learn these and several other terms for a good grade in the course. It is a vocabulary lesson, not a sanctuary for the removal of the greatest external stimuli there is: the presence and power of God in their lives. Again, draw on their personal experience of Jesus and the moral code that HE has written in their heart. Pray together that they may again feel the cleansing power of Jesus and be renewed in the Spirit of their mind. Ask the Lord to rekindle the zeal of faith, bring the praise songs to their minds, and revive the Veggie Tales.

My student's favorite Bible story is: _____

My student's favorite Christian song is: _____

My student can find a simple devotion for the day at: _____

---

**"I have hidden your word in my heart that I might not sin against you." Psalm 119:11**

**"The fear of the Lord is the beginning of wisdom, all who follow His instructions have good insight [...]"**
**Psalm 111:10**

**"In those days there was no king in Israel: every man did that which was right in his own eyes." Judges 21:25**

 *Lord Jesus, the lawless one is again making a play for my child through these teachings. Please touch her in a very real way that she cannot be deceived. Help her to hold on to the moral code that we taught her and the faith that she has known thus far. Let your love pour out upon her and if she has sinned, forgive her and let her know your love.*

We are not rich by what we possess but by what we can do without

# Day 17

## David Hume
### 7 May 1711 - 25 Aug 1776

David Hume's philosophy is, simply stated, "It isn't real unless it happens either to me or from within my 'bundle of emotions.'" And so begins the quest to know our "inner bundle of emotions" or our "true self." So, like the Buddha, we learn to meditate and allow our minds to delve into the questions of suffering and pleasure. We learn yoga and through breathing and fixing our minds on peace we realize a peaceful sensation. Perhaps we find that different substances allow us to tune in better to the inner self so that we can come to reality.

Hume was considered an atheist by both the Catholic and Protestant churches of the day. He liked to tell the story of the best theologian he ever met, an old Edinburgh fish wife, "who having recognized him as Hume the atheist, refused to pull him from the bog into which he had fallen until he declared he was a Christian and repeated the Lord's prayer." In reference to miracles, Hume taught that we should not believe in miracles and that they do not provide us with any reason to think that God exists.

Your student will spend several study hours learning the words and thoughts of this central figure of modernist thought. His teacher, a philosophy major, will statistically be a believer in these words and will live life accordingly. You must be ready to remind your student of the reality of Jesus Christ in his life. Yes, learn it for the paper, but God is and it is He who made us, not we Him.

We teach, "My spirit is the throne room of the most High God, my soul (will, intellect, and emotions) is the instrument upon which He plays His love song to the nations, and my body is the temple of the Holy Spirit." If your child keeps in touch with that, he will not only be significant, he will be a nation-shaper and a world-changer.

My student knew the reality of God at: _____

My student first prayed for someone at: _____

Our video chat key words for this week are <u>clarity</u> and <u>reality</u>.

**"Don't you realize that your body is the temple of the Holy Spirit, who lives in you and was given to you by God?" 1 Corinthians 6:19**

**"These things we also speak, not in words which man's wisdom teaches but which the Holy Spirit teaches, comparing spiritual things with spiritual. But the natural man does not receive the things of the Spirit of God, for they are foolishness to him; nor can he know them, because they are spiritually discerned. But he who is spiritual judges all things, yet he himself is rightly judged by no one." 1 Corinthians 2:13-15**

*Holy Spirit I ask you to reveal to the heart of my child the reality of your wisdom, person, presence, and power. Allow them to sit in these classrooms discerning what is going on, yet not judged by anyone. Allow them the wisdom to see through what is being presented as the lofty thoughts of the ignoble who, denying your existence, fall prey to their own devices. Give my child clarity of thought and mind, lest the fog of humanism affect their soul. Speak to them the things of Jesus.*

# Day 18

## Soren Kierkegaard
### 5 May 1813 – 11 Nov 1855

It will be real when I feel it. The thought of the existentialist is attributed to this modern philosopher. By feelings, we determine what is real and what is not. So, perhaps, you were in worship and the Lord touched you in a way that you began to weep at His wonderful beauty, or to emote in some other way. If Soren was there, then it was real for you, but not for him. So you could not make a universal statement that God is real, because Soren had not had the same experience. He would have no basis for belief.

Relativism says, "it is good for you but not for me." The real question is, why do some people emote one way and others another way? To answer this Kierkegaard examined both the Orthodox and the Unorthodox churches of his day and determined that the church was by man for man. He further concluded that each individual defines "god" in his own way and should not teach or impose his belief on another.

So after a week of reading this philosopher, the student says, "Great for you, but not mine. Do not try to cram your religion down my throat. I never did believe; I only went through the motions to keep you happy. I did it all for you." At this point you have a choice. The pain is very real. The instinct is to drive off the wolf, but old Soren has been dead over 150 years. His words and thoughts live on and have given rise to a horrendous act of rebellion against you and your shared values.

Take a deep breath until laughter at the absurdity of what you have just heard replaces the desire to strangle the voice that said the words. Laugh as though it was a joke and reminisce in the goodness of the memories of worship and night time prayers, of the warmth of Jesus' love and His presence. Do not let the pain get the best of you.

My student knows the real presence of God by: _____

_____

The hearts of the children will be turned: _____ ____ _____

"Having confidence of this very thing, that he who has begun in you a good work will complete it unto Jesus Christ's day." Philippians 1:6

"For indeed Christ died for sins once for all, the Just and Righteous for the unjust and unrighteous." 1 Peter 3:18

"Who being past feeling have given themselves over to lasciviousness, to work all uncleanness with greediness." Ephesians 4:19

*Heavenly Father, please forgive my child for doubting you and your love. In the name of Jesus, I ask you to send warring angels to surround and deliver this child. The wolf is turning his heart against us while your word says the hearts of the children will be turned to the fathers and the fathers to their young. I forgive the pain, rejection, and accusation sown into my child by this course and ask you to protect him from further doubt.*

# Day 19

## *Jean-Paul Sartre*
### *21 June 1905 – 15 April 1980*

Sartre believed that, as humans, people are "condemned to be free." This theory was based upon his belief that there is no Creator. As a teacher of Existentialism, his denial of essence reads this way. If there is no nature breathed in Adam, if he does not receive the breath of God and become a living creature, then he is not different from any other animal. He has no need for redemption, but is the victim of his own choices. There is no handing down of moral code from father to son (his died in his early childhood) or is the church and its teachings to be a father figure in one's life. Each person develops their own moral code based upon their real experiences. Having served in the French army during the war, and having been a POW, he delved deeply into the depth of the emotion of hatred in trying to define if man, who in his thoughts was intrinsically good, could reach the depths of depravity Sartre experienced in war. His book on the hatred of the Jews and explaining how hate operates in men's hearts discusses how hate can be found and eliminated. A communist atheist, Sartre taught and teaches today in our students' classes that existence is at once a blessing and a curse. With no Creator, there is no redeemer for his thought that God was not in Christ redeeming man to himself.

"Illusion has been smashed to bits - martyrdom, salvation and immortality are falling to pieces, the edifice is going to rack and ruin. I collard the Holy Ghost in the basement and threw Him out. Atheism is a cruel and long range affair, I think I have carried it through. I see clearly, I have lost my illusions, I know what my real jobs are."

"We have lost religion, but we have gained humanism. The idea now is to liberate and to help emancipate mankind, with the result that man becomes really an absolute for man."

And there you have the words that lead to "I am not sure of my purpose. I no longer believe that God has a plan for my life. My thoughts are confused and I need to get in touch with my inner self. Perhaps I should leave school until I know what I am to do."

I will encourage my student by: _____

I will strengthen self-worth by: _____

I will suggest an SEAPC Career Link trip to relight the pathway.

**"Then the Lord God formed man from the dust of the ground and breathed into his nostrils the breath or spirit of life, and man became a living being." Genesis 2:7**

**"God was in Christ reconciling the world unto Himself, not counting people's sins against them. And He has committed to us the message of reconciliation." 2 Corinthians 5:19**

**"He breathed on them and said unto them, 'Receive ye the Holy Ghost.'" John 20:22**

*Father, I know that you have been from before the foundations of the earth. You had the thought and spoke the words and by your word all things were made. Jesus is that spoken word. I know that the life essence that dwells in us is made alive by the Holy Spirit. My child is losing sight of this. He is being taught that there is no essence, no God, no Creator, no Redeemer. Holy Spirit, please quicken to him the truth that we have taught him. Please give him again the words of our Lord.*

# Day 20

## Friedrich Nietzsche
### 15 Oct 1844 – 25 Aug 1900

Friedrich Nietzsche was the author of the "God is Dead" theology that resulted in the compromise of the organized church, the emasculation of the body of Christ which was so weak that the Bible could be removed from schools, the Lord's Prayer also removed, and now the mention of Jesus forbidden. It was the question of the post war theology, how could a Christian people behave in such an immoral fashion as to slaughter Jews in Europe, and use nuclear weapons as a threat against other Christian nations? Nietzsche postulated that the behaviors of Christians had actually so undermined the moral principles of the faith that Jesus himself would not recognize the church as His body. If God were dead, killed by the behavior of His called, then absolute truth was also dead so there was no longer an arbitrary, absolute standard for morality. Therefore man had replaced God as divine and as such, could determine his own morality.

Nietzsche, a homosexual who died of syphilis after a complete nervous collapse, is revered in philosophical circles as a man ahead of his times, and given current lifestyles that could be true. From his "The Gay Science" section 125: "God is dead. God remains dead. And we have killed him. How shall we comfort ourselves the murderers of all murderers? What was the holiest and mightiest of all that the world has owned has bled to death under our knives: who will wipe His blood off of us? What water is there for us to clean ourselves? What festivals of atonement, what sacred games shall we have to invent? Is not the greatness of this deed too great for us? Must we ourselves not become gods simply to appear worthy of it?"

In the absence of God, Nietzsche saw a new nihilism, the total darkness of despair in which youth sees no goal, feels massively depressed and follows God in death. When the light of faith, hope, and love is no more, taken away by teachers, peers, and study of these philosophers, suicide becomes a reasonable end to a purposeless life. This is not to strike fear into our hearts as parents, but to cause us to realize the increase in suicides on our nation's campuses and to cover our child from despair and equip them to bring the light of the truth that God is very much alive, and that His word is truth. He loves each and every person in that school and even if they do not believe in Him, or know Him, they can as we agree in prayer and reach out to them.

I will uplift and support my student's life by: _____

_____

My video chat key word is: _____

The scripture verse for today is: _____

_____

**"Let not your heart be troubled. You believe in God, believe also in me. In my Father's house there are many mansions. If not, I would have told you: because I go to prepare a place for you." John 14:1**

**"Jesus said to him, I am the way, the truth, and the life: no man comes to the Father, but by me." John 14:6**

**"I am come that they may have life, and may have it more abundantly." John 10:10**

 *God, I know you are alive for you live in me. Please protect my child from this anti-Christ teaching that you are dead. I can feel your presence as I pray. I know you hear me when I call. Please watch over these children as they have to learn these terrible words. Help them to strengthen each other and encourage one another in the faith.*

# Day 21

## *Equipping Options for You*

We have now been three weeks together in prayer and the word of God concerning the pathway for your child. Hopefully this last section on philosophy has brought back some of the education you received or has made clear the words and thoughts your student has been learning and explained some of the new words and emotions you are hearing in your communication times. Today we want to look at some promises of equipping and ways to pray as we launch into the fourth section of this prayer guide.

We are at best wrestling for the student, and at worst, in full-fledged warfare. We must be gentle, steady, positive, and loving in our approach as we see the manifestation of the mental and emotional struggles through which they are going. It is difficult to see your child adapt language and appearance to conform to a new location and culture. One college freshman reported to her father, who is a pastor, that the most difficult, distasteful thing for her was the language that students used; she had never used or heard such vulgarity.

The apostle, Paul, in his second letter to the church at Corinth, the philosophy center, commented that, "For the weapons of our warfare are not carnal but mighty in God for pulling down strongholds, casting down arguments and every high thing that exalts itself against the knowledge of God, bringing every thought into captivity to the obedience of Christ," (2 Corinthians 10:4-5).

Your student is going to use you as a sounding board for the arguments he is learning. The thoughts have become words and those words have to be tested. Thank God He has given us His Word with which to pull down these arguments. Stay calm, love the person, and be clear in what the word says. Do not attack the teacher, but listen for the key words of the philosophers and respond with the word of God.

Each of these philosophers lost a parent or was rejected at an early age. Their denial of Christ and the church is growing out of their own pain. Remind your child of the good things the Lord has done for them. Fill their minds with acceptance, cleansing, and forgiveness. Remember, the words that follow "you are" are the most important words you will share with them.

"Let the word of Christ dwell in you richly in all wisdom; teaching and admonishing one another in psalms and hymns and spiritual songs, singing with grace in your hearts to the Lord." Colossians 3:16

"And take the helmet of salvation, and the sword of the Spirit, which is the Word of God" Ephesians 6:17

"I do not pray that You should take them out of the world, but that You should keep them from the evil one." John 17:15

*Father I pray for the anointing of the Holy Spirit to bring back to my mind your word as I talk with my child. I pray that the love I have for them and your greater love would flow through me. I stand against any argument that denies Christ and You. I pray that the power of your word, not my emotions will carry the day in this discussion. I pray that my child will wear the helmet of his salvation to protect his mind from the world's ways and that your word will dwell within him always.*

# Humanism

# Humanism

The philosophers became lecturers and writers. Realizing that books are stronger than bullets and that the pen is more powerful than the sword they taught their message of no God, no creation, no biblical truth over 3 centuries until the 20th century by which time the educational community and the western church were ready to throw off the restraints of a biblical moral standard. By the death of Sartre in April of 1980, the Bible and prayer and the mention of Jesus had been removed from public education and the Ten Commandments from most public buildings. Ivy League schools that had been intended to train preachers had become bastions of the new educational philosophy.

Launched in the United Kingdom as Secular Humanism (the quest for the Absolute Man), and developed in the United States, the Humanist movement gained great speed.

With the fear of God gone, and the Bible and Jesus removed, the Supreme Court became the body of man to determine morality. So truth, rather than being instituted by the thoughts and words and enforced by the actions of God became a series of decisions reached through discussion by this appointed group. Now man was in control of what is right and what is wrong.

The Civil Rights movement, promoted as a way to bring equality to all men regardless of color or creed, soon evolved into greater rights for the whites and left the black man mired in a new form of slavery: compromised education, unequal opportunity for career advancement, and violent culture behaviors and habits.

Having thrown off the restraints of God and the Church, the court decided that men should marry men and women should marry women, and that unwanted infants could be destroyed before birth and their body parts sold for research. The court will decide when life begins and when life ends.

It is into this Humanistic world that your student is thrust and as they listen to hour after hour of the vocabulary of this culture, their faith is eroded.

If you do not take the time and effort to communicate biblical, Christ-centered values, and a Christian world view to your child, then you cannot be amazed at what you find them to be in 4 to 6 years.

Prayer is the most wonderful, loving thing you can do. Having at your ready a Bible-based, loving, non-confrontational, apologetic steeped in their own testimonies of things God has done for them, how Jesus is real to them and how they are very special to Him is the best antidote for the virus to which they are being exposed. You must make visits to that campus, take your student to lunch or dinner and listen to what they say to you. Video chatting on a tablet or smartphone is essential. Phone calls for just a few minutes are vital.

Yes, they have to learn the words to get the degree. And once they have mastered those words, they will be equipped to be a voice for Christ in their generation.

For the next seven days we will look at the seven principals of the Amsterdam Declaration, the "Stone Tablets" of humanism. And we will pray that a generation will pull them down and return to a loving God

# Day 22

## Humanism is Ethical

"Humanism is ethical. It affirms the worth, dignity and autonomy of the individual and the right of every human being to the greatest possible freedom compatible with the rights of others. Humanists have a duty of care to all of humanity including future generations. Humanists believe that morality is an intrinsic part of human nature based on understanding and a concern for others, needing no external sanction." *The Amsterdam Declaration 2002*

Ethics is a moral philosophy. Without God or any other "external sanction" the individual is free to be self-determinate and to defend their personal right. The thought is that they will stop any acts, behaviors, or habits and control any emotions that cross a line called "concern for others." It would be great if it was true that human nature, without a Divine intervention, had any concern for others. But history has proven that man left to his own devices will destroy himself and the decline of Europe, the UK, and now the US proves that our ethics require an arbitrary sanction of God.

The campus life and its leaders repeat a mantra of thoughts, words, emotions, actions, and behaviors that have become habits. The result is "ethical" in that the word "ethics" derives from the Greek word for "habits" so "everybody does it" becomes an ethical norm. Morals go down the drain as the student learns the thoughts and words that throw off the governance of the Creator and the freedom of the Redeemer. It takes four years to accomplish the indoctrination of the students to the humanistic way of thought, words, actions, and ethics. By six years they have mastered the process and teach in public schools without prayer, the Bible, Christian songs or any expression of an external sanction sowing the thoughts and words into the minds of defenseless children who then justify as ethical behaviors that destroy.

You and your child are going to be instruments of righteousness on your campus. You are going to pray and invoke the power of the Holy Spirit onto the campus. You are going to daily encourage your student to question the thoughts and words as to their outcomes in history. If not in the classroom for fear of certain retaliation, then in their own thoughts and with fellow students and campus ministries.

**"Now it shall come to pass, if you diligently obey the voice of the Lord your God, to observe carefully all His commandments which I command you today, that the Lord your God will set you high above all nations of the earth." Deuteronomy 28:1**

Read the first 14 verses of the chapter and pray for your student and family.

**"Blessed is the man who fears the Lord, who delights greatly in His commandments. His descendants will be mighty on the earth; The generation of the upright will be blessed." Psalm 112:1-2**

**"This is my commandment, that you love one another as I have loved you." John 15:12**

 *Lord Jesus, please forgive us for allowing humanism to overtake our generation. We as a people have thrown off your restraints and everyone cries for liberty but in man there is none. Please forgive our sin and heal our land. I pray for my child that he will not be ensnared in these humanistic thought but will rise above and maintain his Godly world view. Give me the words to counteract these humanistic words.*

# Day 23

## Humanism is Rational

"Humanism is rational. It seeks to use science creatively, not destructively. Humanists believe that the solutions to the world's problems lie in human thought and action rather than divine intervention. Humanism advocates the application of the methods of science and free inquiry to the problems of human welfare. But Humanists also believe that the application of science and technology must be tempered by human values. Science gives us the means but human values must propose the ends." *The Amsterdam Declaration 2002*

If there is no God and if there are no miracles, then why would we have to state that He cannot solve the problems of man who He created? Oh, yes, humanists also believe there was not creation, nor that man is the highest form of animals and not carrying the essence of the Creator, but that the human nature has also evolved from the instincts of apes.

Humanism then says that there is no place for starting the school day or any day with prayer. Margaret Sanger, the mother of Planned Parenthood and Humanist of the Year in 1957 must have an interesting rationale for the application of science to be tempered by human values. Perhaps she had never seen a woman give birth or any other animal for that matter. The inconsistencies here are so obvious that the student must be under a fog of charm or pseudo-intellectualism to be able to read the materials and master the vocabulary.

That is why the "no God and no prayer" principles are invoked at an early age. Once your student has had a personal encounter with Jesus, they are going to mentally stand and not accept these words. The campus ministry is there to refresh their Christian vocabulary through worship and conversation that is Christ centered. They have graduated from universities and have a special call from the Lord to minister in the midst of this battle for minds.

Please contact a student ministry on your student's campus and arrange for them to meet your student. It could be the best call you make.

My student understands the meaning of love the Lord first and love humanity second.

I will reignite the fire of daily prayers by: _____

_____

My prayer time is: _____

**"Yahweh, your word is settled in heaven forever. Your faithfulness is to all generations. You have established the earth, and it remains." Psalm 119:89-90**

**"Call to Me, and I will answer you, and show you great and mighty things, which you do not know." Jeremiah 33:3**

**"When he calls out to me, I will answer him. I will be with him when he is in trouble; I will rescue him and bring him honor." Psalm 91:15**

 *Oh Lord God you have made the heavens and the earth. You have spoken and we were formed. Now the people are given over to a fantasy that you do not exist and there is no prayer. Because we do not acknowledge your Lordship in the morning, classrooms are chaotic. Lord, forgive us. Reignite the fire for prayer in my heart and lead me to a good campus ministry partner or my child. Make the way of rescue for us.*

# Day 24

## Humanism Supports Democracy & Human Rights

"Humanism supports democracy and human rights. Humanism aims at the fullest possible development of every human being. It holds that democracy and human development are matters of right. The principles of democracy and human rights can be applied to many human relationships and are not restricted to methods of government." *The Amsterdam Declaration 2002*

The focus is human rights as opposed to civil rights. The humanist philosophy directs its declaration away from the democratic civil code that provides equal rights under the law to all who have pledged allegiance to the United States of America and to the republic: One nation, under God, with liberty and justice for all. This declaration is talking about human relationships. So marriage is not a covenant between a man and a woman, because that biblical ethical and moral norm has been replaced with a new, modern, and more enlightened understanding of humanity. Upheld by the Supreme Court and now the law of the land, elementary school books are already printed presenting children with homosexual, bisexual, and transgender relationships as morally correct. During the debate before the court, the civil rights movement was set forth as an example of constitutional precedent for the relational rights sought by the LGBT lawyers. Of course, the humanist court found in favor of the humanist agenda and we live with the results.

Universities are the place in American culture where new norms are investigated, discussed, and each student is given the time for thought and discussion to determine how they feel about such issues. They learn the words of political correctness and situational ethics and make a determination of where they stand on these issues and all issues of life. The more emotional protest others' positions and proclaim the virtue of their own. This creates a forum for discussion which the Humanist feels is going to get to the truth on an issue. Speakers and special teachers are brought in for open forum discussion and ideals are formed. Very few of these speakers are from the Christian community either by their choice or that of the university. So, in the campus culture, your student and the campus ministry are the voice for Christ. Not the Christianity of history, but the now faith. The relationship of love and forgiveness that removes shame and gives grace. The joy of simplicity in a very convoluted world. Encourage your student to gently and lovingly present an apologetic that involves a real, personal experience with Christ.

> **"So, as much as is in me, I am ready to preach the gospel to you who are in Rome also. For I am not ashamed of the gospel of Christ, for it is the power of God to salvation for everyone who believes, for the Jew first and also for the Greek. For in it the righteousness of God is revealed from faith to faith; as it is written, 'The just shall live by faith.'"**
> **Romans 1:15-17**

> **"Therefore God also gave them up in the lusts of their hearts to uncleanness, that their bodies should be dishonored among themselves, who exchanged the truth of God for a lie, and worshiped and served the creature rather than the Creator, who is blessed forever. Amen. For this reason, God gave them up to vile passions. For their women changed the natural function into that which is against nature. Likewise also the men, leaving the natural function of the woman, burned in their lust toward one another, men doing what is inappropriate with men, and receiving in themselves the due penalty of their error."**
> **Romans 1:24-27**

*Father, in the Name of Jesus I pray that you will forgive us for abandoning the righteousness of the gospel and condoning that which you detest. I pray that my child will not make the exchange and that she may be a light in the midst. That she will stand for virtue and be true to you. I pray that through her you will release wisdom and signs and wonders. Bring her to fellowship that believes in you and experiences the presence of the Holy Spirit.*

# Day 25

## *Humanism Imposes No Dogma or Creed*

"Humanism insists that personal liberty must be combined with social responsibility.Humanism ventures to build a world on the idea of the free person responsible to society, and recognises our dependence on and responsibility for the natural world. Humanism is undogmatic, imposing no creed upon its adherents. It is thus committed to education free from indoctrination." *The Amsterdam Declaration 2002*

So, here is the issue your student is facing as they dialogue concerning Humanism or Faith, if society sets a norm of behavior in which your student is uncomfortable, are they under social pressure to join in or face shunning by the society? It hasn't worked well for the Amish and the Mennonites.

Humanistic societal policing comes first in the form of political correctness in word selection. Why is that such a big deal if the individual has not crossed a physical line? Are we not free to express our thoughts in words? They may lead to emotions, but not to actions if we are under control. So if the goal is to not be dogmatic, and to encourage free speech, then why would a person be avoided if they believed in God, talked about Jesus, read their Bible, and presented a Christian would view?

Because thoughts become words which lead to actions and behaviors and to preserve the humanistic, non-god culture, such thought should not be allowed nor entertained. If that is not indoctrination, then what is?

The repression of Christian faith through classroom discourse has been reported on every major university campus in America. Your student will need your support, the support of a campus fellowship and a lot of prayer to be able to understand the thoughts and words of the culture, but not be forced into buying into it. The non-god agenda is in every department and in each classroom. If your child went to a Christian school, they will now be severely tested in all they have learned. They will need the support of former teachers and classmates. Encourage social media connections and work for them to stand.

Prayer is the most powerful weapon you have. Take time to pray. Ask others to pray. Get a prayer chain of parents of university students to stand together in prayer for this generation.

My local prayer partners are: _____

_____

I will support my student's declaration of Christ by strengthening my own.

**"Again I say to you that if two of you agree on earth concerning anything that they ask, it will be done for them by My Father in heaven." Matthew 18:19**

**"Blessed are you when they revile and persecute you, and say all kinds of evil against you falsely for My sake. Rejoice and be exceedingly glad, for great is your reward in heaven, for so they persecuted the prophets who were before you." Matthew 5:11-12**

 *Jesus, no one likes to be shunned. You came to your own and they did not receive you. Please give grace to stand to my child. Please give them the strength in fellowship to be a light in the midst of darkness.*

# Day 26

## *Humanism is a Response*

"Humanism is a response to the widespread demand for an alternative to dogmatic religion. The world's major religions claim to be based on revelations fixed for all time, and many seek to impose their world-views on all of humanity. Humanism recognises that reliable knowledge of the world and ourselves arises through a continuing process. of observation, evaluation and revision." *The Amsterdam Declaration 2002*

I am not too sure that my Muslim, Buddhist, and Hindu friends would enjoy this declaration. The Jews with whom we work in medical projects would certainly question the use of the word "widespread." For something to be an alternative to dogmatic religion there would have to be a dogmatic religion to which it could compare itself. Not even the Orthodox Church from which the philosophical fathers of humanism fled could any longer be called dogmatic. If anything, it has been reformed to a point of inclusion of all except for the cherished sacraments. Both the Lutheran and Catholic churches have open communion as does the Church of England so the point of dogma is a bit ancient.

Do young people hunger for a feeling of love and support, of forgiveness and understanding, of acceptance and unconditional love? For sure they do and in increasing numbers they are finding this and more in the development of a personal relationship with Jesus. Your student brings Christ to the campus and can be used of the Lord to save, heal, and deliver other young people from the "alternative culture."

In their first classes they are going to meet people of like faith. Relationships will build and they can get into fellowship in the word and prayer. Great movements have begun on university campuses and your student can be the one God uses to spark a flame that will bright across the land. Your prayers for protection will create a platform for Christian maturity and the lives they touch will go into all the professions resulting in a generation that seeks and serves the Lord.

If humanists are at all correct, they are seeing a spiritual hunger in the land. They are hearing a heart cry aimed at heaven. No human thought or philosophy will satisfy this heart cry. There will be a great student Christian movement on campuses across America and because you are praying, your child will be a part of it.

My student will meet _____

from _____ campus ministries.

I will share prayer direction with my student.

> **"If My people who are called by My name will humble themselves, and pray and seek My face, and turn from their wicked ways, then I will hear from heaven, and will forgive their sin and heal their land." 2 Chronicles 7:14**
>
> **"And it shall come to pass in the last days, says God, That I will pour out of My Spirit on all flesh; Your sons and your daughters shall prophesy," Acts 2:17**
>
> **"Jesus answered and said to him, 'If anyone loves Me, he will keep My word; and My Father will love him, and We will come to him and make Our home with him.'" John 14:23**

*Father, I believe this is the generation that will take your name into all the earth. Please pour out your Spirit on my child and their friends, sons and daughters. Let them see visions and dreams and speak for you. Give them wisdom to know the times and your word for their generation.*

# Day 27

## *Humanism Values the Arts and Creativity*

"Humanism values artistic creativity and imagination and recognises the transforming power of art. Humanism affirms the importance of literature, music, and the visual and performing arts for personal development and fulfilment." *The Amsterdam Declaration 2002*

Creativity is a confirmation of the God essence in man. If all humans have an innate creative capacity, then they would have to have had a common origin. There would be no uniqueness in voice or perspective, for all man would be the same. However, each person is a uniquely crafted gift from God to mankind for its betterment. When these gifts are returned to the Lord as praise or worship, they flourish. When they are not, the artist goes mad, the musician overdoses, and violence invades the tapestry.

This violent behavior, the dark side, will increase only as light is removed. Students who are walking away from the culture of righteousness, peace, and joy in the Holy Spirit begin to have a shadow in their eyes. This is one reason why we strongly suggest you invest in the technology and training to be able to have face time with your student. You want to see those eyes. Considering your investment in tuition, room, and board, two tablets and the necessary software cannot be that much of an expense.

Face to face time is the best and your appreciation of song, dramatic endeavor, and music is essential to the continuation of your close relationship with your student. Watch over the investment you are making. Encourage them to use the God-given talent to glorify Him and keep a regular eye to eye appointment.

My student first drew: _____

My student's first play was: _____

My student's first song was: _____

"Therefore He says: 'When He ascended on high, He led captivity captive, And gave gifts to men.'" Ephesians 4:8

"Praise the Lord! Praise God in His sanctuary; praise Him
　　in his mighty firmament!
Praise Him for His mighty acts; praise him for His
　　excellent greatness!
Praise Him with the sound of the trumpet; praise Him
　　with the lute and harp!
Praise Him with the timbrel and dance; praise Him with
　　stringed instruments and flutes!
Praise Him with loud cymbals; praise Him with clashing
　　cymbals!
Let everything that has breath praise the Lord." Psalm 150

*Father, you have given special gifts to my child. I recognize that they are given to praise you and to uplift the hearts of those around them. Please help my child to carry these gifts with humility and excellence. Develop these gifts and talents for your glory, in Jesus' name.*

# Day 28

## *Humanism is a Life Stance*

Humanism is a life stance aiming at the maximum possible fulfillment through the cultivation of ethical and creative living and offering an ethical and rational means of addressing the challenges of our time. Humanism can be a way of life for everyone everywhere.

Life stance is the word to replace world view. Christians see the world from the point of view of the Creator, the love of the Redeemer, and the sustaining power of the Holy Spirit. The love of God is demonstrated in His provision of the elements necessary to platform God given success. His person, purpose, and plan are central to the events on the earth and cannot be separated from them. He manifests His love in daily provision.

Life stance is world view without God and His paternal power. It is self-established. It is humankind saying to the Creator, "I no longer need you or want you in my life." It is Adam hiding in the garden. It is Cain asking if he is his brother's keeper in the first test of humanism.

Life stance says "there is no sin so I do not need a Redeemer. I can, through my intellect, make choices that offer me habits and logic to resolve my own issues, make my own rules, and determine reality without the intervention or interference of a god or higher power. I am a free moral agent capable of creating my own reason and ethic."

Life stance says "there is no hope in divine intervention or place for prayer. Since there is no God, there is no way of need to talk to Him, so I will just work it out on my own. I will think every problem through and deal with it in my way. I will develop my own moral compass and live accordingly. I will determine what is and what ought to be and make what ought to be what is in my life." Or, as President Clinton once said, "It depends on what the meaning of the word 'is' is."

My student expresses a Christian world view by: _____

_____

My student is no fool.

> **"The fool has said in his heart, 'There is no God.' They
> are corrupt, They have done abominable works, There is
> none who does good. The Lord looks down from heaven
> upon the children of men, To see if there are any who
> understand, who seek God. They have all turned aside,
> They have together become corrupt; There is none who
> does good, No, not one." Psalm 14:1-3**

*Father, in the name of Jesus let your longsuffering be greater
than your anger. Help me to help my child continue in a Christian
world view understanding and feeling your love. Help me, Lord
to bring to him the understanding that there is a God, you have a
Son, and Jesus died for us. Help him to understand your sustaining
love for the world. Help him Lord to seek your will in all things
and to use your word as the standard for his rational in every
circumstance. Love him Lord, and forgive his sins.*

# Continuing the Journey

# Continuing the Journey

So, we have prayed together and learned from the Lord several things. Now the forever question is, "What to do?"

On these next few pages, I am going to encourage you to take a very proactive role in the education years of your student. As a young adult, they want to make their own decisions and test the waters of life. That is fine, but your role as an intercessor for them has not changed. You want to keep in touch, speak the Biblical words of a Christian culture and world view into their young adult mind, and pray daily if not several times a day.

Thank God for video chatting and social media. These enable us to be in regular communication with our sons and daughters as they navigate campus and make decisions on career. We can see their faces, hear their voices and can be very clear with them concerning a bigger picture in which to frame their futures. Communication is the life blood of relationship, so make every effort at continuing communication.

This is where you can use your non-confrontational, gentle, prayer-soaked apologetic to gently remind your student of the reality of Christ in their lives. Their relationships are changing, and they're experiencing new things, new thoughts and new words, but you are still the most important voice in their lives. Steadily through prayer and your love for them, you will be able to guide them through the changes. Just as you could not make them little forever, neither can you hold them now. Their kite will fly, but you can be the tail that keeps them stable.

We are encouraging you to make regular visits to the campus. Walk and pray there. Our book, *The Attack Lambs* would be a good guide for this mobile prayer. As you walk, you will see hundreds of young people, the future of the nation. It is for them that we encourage you to pray, love, and gently guide. You will find them to be wonderfully kind if you get lost on campus. They may be a bit distracted with their phones, but give grace, they might be talking with their own mother or father.

With whatever opportunity the Lord gives you, try to introduce your student to campus ministries. We have included a list of the websites of several of these. Just contact them to find out the name of their representative on your campus and attempt to make the connection. Your child is most likely over 18, so the choice is theirs and the ministry is often times not supposed to approach them. One of the rules of the new culture, this can be overcome by a simple introductory email, text, or lunch on your part. Just so the two points for contact are identified, then you can watch the Lord move.

These four years are an adventure for sure, but they can be the most significant and wonderfully rewarding as you watch that young person walk down that aisle, receive that diploma, and move that tassel. We are praying and believing with you for the happiest possible transition through these years.

If we can be of service to you, please do not hesitate to contact us at www.seapc.org.

# Day 29

## *Prayer for Campuses*

In many documented cases, focused prayer for campuses has seen an increase in student ministries and a decrease in violent crime. Though the administrators of universities run the risk of censure and job loss, the parents of students at that university have no such considerations. You can go over there and pray and call upon the Lord all day. In many places you cannot stand up and preach, but you can answer questions.

We at SEAPC encourage and lead prayer teams to campuses and take a prayer walk around the place. We visit the administration buildings, the student unions, the science and philosophy departments, and the fraternity row. We find out if there is a mosque in the campus as well as churches and we visit and pray. We interview students, gaining the type of information with which we are equipping you. For the most part we find a very intelligent, communicative generation who has a dream of significance. Many, but not all, have no Christian testimony. They talk of home and the church, but did not have a personal encounter with Jesus. On the whole, they appreciate the opportunity they have and are trying hard to make the best of it.

We are very upbeat about what we find. From Harvard Square to Cal-San Diego we have spoken with young people and are encouraged to find a hunger in them for Spiritual truth. As they encounter the Spirit of Truth who will lead them in all truth, they become an amazingly intelligent group who we feel will forge the future of the nation and the world. We are very excited to partner with the recommended campus ministries to help guide these young people to fulfillment in the plan Jesus has for them.

We encourage you to make frequent visits to a campus near you. Walk on the grounds and pray for what you see. Ask the Lord to open the eyes of your understanding and give you wisdom in the knowledge of His purpose and power for that place. Sit where students and faculty pass by and look at them and pray for them. Jesus knows their past and future, the number of hairs on their heads and the thought and intents of their hearts. Sit there and pray. Eyes wide open, head lifted up, gazing upon the people for they are indeed like sheep without a shepherd. Find the campus ministry and connect with them. Let them know that you and your group of prayer warriors are standing with them for a visitation of God to their campus. Find out about outreaches and short term opportunities. Just stopping in to see them will bring great encouragement. Walk that campus and claim it for Jesus. Believe the promise to Joshua, "Every place upon which the sole of your foot shall tread, that have I given to you."

**"Every place upon which the sole of your foot shall tread, that have I given to you." Joshua 1:3**

**"But when He saw the multitudes, He was moved with compassion for them, because they were weary and scattered, like sheep having no shepherd. Then He said to His disciples, 'The harvest truly is plentiful, but the laborers are few. Therefore pray the Lord of the harvest to send out laborers into His harvest.'" Matthew 9:36-38**

*Father, Lord of the Harvest, I give myself to you to be an instrument of prayer. Please send laborers to harvest these young people. Show me my part in supporting campus ministries and how my child can be used in this great generation.*

# Day 30

## *A Question of Authority*

So, if my child becomes a university student, do I still have authority in their life? When are they ready to make their own choices? For how long can I reach out to them without smothering them? Where is the balance of trust and control? Am I cramming my faith down their throat? How much freedom is too much? Do I have to pay for a life stance with which I do not agree? How can I keep from losing my child to the new culture? Are the two cultures compatible in any areas?

As far as the campus goes, there are rules that are designed for public and student safety. There are also those who intentionally break the rules to take advantage of naive students. A false sense of security is worse than no security at all. You need to take a campus tour and locate several things for your prayer list. You need to know the administration building and who your contact person is there. You need to know the dorm or other housing arrangement and walk through the place to see how you feel in it. See if you feel at risk in the place or if you feel comfortable.

Check the same way on roommates and "first friends." Ask the awkward questions up front so you do not have to deal with more awkward situations down the road. Walk from the library and student union to the housing area. See how you feel as you quietly stroll along. Remember every place your foot will tread, the Lord will give it to you. Yes, it may seem a bit overboard to actually case the place, but you are gathering information for prayer and communication with your number one investment.

Discover the online pathway to know your child's schedule, class selection, professors, and texts. Pray over these with a whole heart. They are the places and times that the words of a new culture are going to be spoken into your child's soul. Cover that kid with prayer. Recite to the Lord the hopes and promises you have for the child and communicate encouragement to them. Participate in the developmental process. Prayer involvement is essential to the spiritual condition of your student. Locate and connect with a campus ministry. Pray for and support their outreach. Encourage them to meet your child and encourage your child to give them a chance. There is a place suited for your student. As you pray, the Lord will lead you to the right connections for He loves that kid more than you ever will.

Your child is living on a cultural battlefield. They must be supported as a soldier would be. Having the courage to withstand the words of the enemy, they must be supported in prayer.

**"Arise, walk through the length and the breadth of the land, for I will give it to you." Genesis 13:17**

**"His offspring will be mighty in the land; the generation of the upright will be blessed." Psalm 112:2**

**"And lead us not into temptation, but deliver us from evil." Matthew 6:13**

*Father, in the name of Jesus, I thank you that my child will be one of those you use to lead his generation in paths of righteousness. He will be mighty in the land. I thank you for my child and for your hand of protection and guiding voice in his life.*

# Glossary of Terms*

ABSOLUTE: Something that is independent of, and unconditioned by, anything external to itself (non-contingent).

ABSTRACT IDEA: A general idea; that which exists in the mind rather than in the external world.

ABSURD: In logic, that which is irrational or contradictory.

ACCIDENT: In metaphysics, a quality, property or characteristic that is not essential to the nature of a thing.

ACTUALITY: In scholastic philosophy, the state of being something in reality (or in fact) rather than being something in potential.

AD HOC: Literally, to or for this; pertaining to this one particular case alone.

AD INFINITUM: Going on forever (without end).

AESTHETICS: The branch of philosophy concerned with the study of beauty and art.

A FORTIORI: Literally, with greater force; in logic, all the more reason.

AGNOSTICISM: The belief that one does not, or cannot, know ultimate reality (especially God).

ALTRUISM: The belief that everyone should be concerned for the benefit and welfare of others.

AMORAL: That which is neither moral nor immoral; outside the moral realm.

ANALYTIC PHILOSOPHY: A modern movement in philosophy (primarily in England and North America) which identifies the analysis of language as the central task of philosophy. Linguistic analysis is used as a tool to identify and resolve philosophical problems.

ANALYTIC PROPOSITION: According to Kant, a proposition (statement) that is true by definition; a proposition whose predicate is deducible from the subject, as in "All bachelors are unmarried men."

ANGST: A German term for an inner sense of despair or dread.

ANTHROPOMORPHISM: The act of ascribing human characteristics to non-humans (especially to God).

* written by Ken Samples at http://www.str.org/articles/100-basic-philosophic-terms#.Vuw2EPkrLIU

ANTHROPOMORPHISM: The act of ascribing human characteristics to non-humans (especially to God).

ANTINOMY: A contradiction made up of a thesis and antithesis.

ANTITHESIS: The contrast or opposite of the thesis statement.

APOLOGETICS: Literally, to give a defense; in philosophy, to give rational justification for one's beliefs.

A POSTERIORI: In epistemology, knowledge derived from, or posterior to (comes after), five sense experience. Knowledge that comes from experience.

A PRIORI: In epistemology, knowledge which is acquired prior to, or independently of, five sense experience.

ARCHETYPE: An original model, type, pattern, or paradigm.

ARISTOTELIANISM: Of or pertaining to the philosophy of Aristotle (384-322 B.C.)

ATHEISM: The belief that no God or gods exist in or beyond the universe (traditional usage). Sometimes defined as an absence of belief in God.

ATTRIBUTE: A quality, property, or characteristic which is attributed to, or predicated of, something.

AUGUSTINIANISM: Of or pertaining to the philosophical and theological thought of St. Augustine (354-430).

AUTONOMY: The state of being independent, self-determining, or free.

AXIOLOGY: The branch of philosophy concerned with the study of values.

BEING: That which exists, or is real (unchanging reality).

CATEGORICAL IMPERATIVE: Immanuel Kant's central ethical principle of conduct: "Always act so as to will the maxim of your action to become a universal law." Moral conduct should be universalized. The classic example of a purely deontological approach to ethics.

CAUSALITY, PRINCIPLE OF: Every effect must have a sufficient cause; everything that comes into being must have a cause.

COHERENCE THEORY OF TRUTH: Truth is determined by that which is internally and logically consistent.

CONTINGENT: The state of being dependent upon something else for existence.

CORRESPONDENCE THEORY OF TRUTH: Truth is determined by that which corresponds to the present state of affairs.

**COSMOLOGICAL ARGUMENT:** A proof for the existence of God; derived from the Greek word kosmos (world), the argument states that a contingent world requires the existence of God as its ultimate cause. The argument appears in different forms (unmoved mover, first cause, contingency, kalam), and has been presented and defended by numerous philosophers including: Aristotle, Thomas Aquinas, Gottfried Leibniz, and Medieval Islamic philosopher Al-Ghazali.

**COSMOS:** From the Greek word kosmos, meaning world or universe.

**DEDUCTIVE REASONING:** Reasoning in which the conclusion of an argument follows with logical necessity (certainty) from the premises. Deductive Reasoning usually proceeds from general to particular, or from whole to parts. Contrasted with Inductive Reasoning.

**DEISM:** Belief in a God who created the world, but does not intervene within it (God is transcendent, but not immanent). This religious world view, which emphasizes reason over revelation, was most popular during the 17th and 18th centuries in England, France and America.

**DETERMINISM:** The view that everything in the universe is controlled by previous conditions, and therefore could not be otherwise.

**DIALECTIC:** The process of drawing out logical truths through dialogue, reasoning and argumentation.

**DOUBT:** From the Latin dubito, to be uncertain.

**DUALISM:** In metaphysics, the view that reality consists of two fundamentally distinct entities.

**EFFICIENT CAUSE:** The agent through which something is produced or comes into being.

**EMPIRICISM:** The belief that the source of all knowledge is five sense experience. All knowledge of actually existing things is acquired through five sense experience. Contrasted with Rationalism.

**EPICUREANISM:** A hedonistic philosophy, founded by Epicurus, which stressed long-term and higher pleasure (i.e., pleasures of the mind over the bodily appetites).

**EPISTEMOLOGY:** The branch or field of philosophy concerned with the origin, nature, and limits of knowledge.

**ESSENCE:** The nature or "whatness" of a thing. The qualities or attributes hat make a thing what it is.

**ETHICS:** The branch or field of philosophy concerned with moral values and human conduct.

**EXISTENTIALISM:** A modern approach (movement) to philosophy which rejects abstractions, and stresses concrete reality, especially individual human freedom, choice, subjectivity, and existence.

**FIDEISM:** The view that there is no way (and often no need) to justify one's beliefs (usually religious belief). It is usually asserted that faith alone is sufficient.

FINAL CAUSE: For the sake of which an agent acts (i.e., the end or goal). One of Aristotle's four causes.

FINITE: Having specific boundaries, limitations, or an end. Limitations in attributes and character. Considered the opposite of infinite.

FORM: In metaphysics, the essence or nature of an entity.

FORMAL CAUSE: The structure, form, pattern, or configuration of which something consists. One of Aristotle's four causes.

FOUNDATIONALISM: In epistemology, the belief that all knowledge is based upon first principles (foundational truths) which provide justification for all other beliefs. Some would argue that these foundational truths are themselves not subject to any proof.

HEDONISM: The ethical viewpoint which asserts that pleasure is the summum bonum (greatest good). It is often asserted that mankind is a pleasure-seeking, pain-avoiding animal. There have been several different types of hedonistic philosophies (e.g., Epicureanism, Egoism, Utilitarianism, etc.).

HUMANISM: The view that "mankind is the measure of all things." Something's value or significance is measured by its relationship to mankind.

IDEALISM: The metaphysical view that all reality consists of mind and/or ideas. Contrasted with Materialism.

IMMANENT: The state of being present with something (e.g., God is immanent [present within the universe]).

INDEPENDENT: In Metaphysics, existence that is not conditioned or controlled by something external to itself; a non-contingent.

INDETERMINISM: The view that at least some events, especially the human will and behavior, are free of causal determination.

INDUBITABLE: Beyond all doubt; absolutely or unquestionably true.

INDUCTIVE REASONING: Reasoning in which the conclusion of an argument follows only probably from the premises. Inductive Reasoning usually proceeds from particular to general, or from parts to whole. Contrasted with Deductive Reasoning.

INFINITE: Without boundaries, limitations, or an end. No limitations in attributes or character. Considered the opposite of finite.

INNATE IDEAS: The belief that at least some ideas are inborn (i.e., present in the mind at birth).

INTUITION: The faculty by which truth is immediately grasped, separate from five sense experience or reason.

LOGIC: The study of the principles of correct thinking. The science that evaluates thinking and argumentation. Considered a major branch or field of philosophy.

MATERIAL CAUSE: The matter, stuff, or substance of which something is made. One of Aristotle's four causes.

MATERIALISM: The metaphysical view that all reality consists of material or physical entities with their physical properties. Contrasted with Idealism.

METAPHYSICS: The branch or field of philosophy concerned with the ultimate nature, structure, and characteristics of reality. A narrow usage of the term refers to the study of that which lies beyond the physical realm (i.e., the supernatural realm). Metaphysics is sometimes used interchangeably with the term Ontology.

MONISM: The metaphysical view that all reality is one. Idealism and Materialism are examples of monism.

MORAL ARGUMENT: A proof for the existence of God; God's existence is the only adequate grounds to explain objective morality.

NATURALISM: The belief that physical nature is the only reality. The philosophy of naturalism is characterized by Monism, antisupernaturalism, scientism, and Humanism.

NIHILISM: The view that there is no meaning, purpose, significance, or value in the universe.

NOETIC: Pertaining to reason, knowledge, and the intellect.

NOUMENA: In Kant, the thing-in-itself, the world as it really is, apart from its appearance; as opposed to the phenomena (the world of appearance). Also referred to as the "noumenon" or "noumenal world."

OBJECTIVE IDEALISM: The belief that things (ideas) genuinely exist apart from our perception of them.

OCKHAM'S RAZOR: The explanation which fits the facts with the least assumptions is the best. Also know as the principle of parsimony.

ONTOLOGICAL ARGUMENT: A proof for the existence of God; St. Anselm argued that reflection on God's perfect essence (or being) actually necessitates His existence.

ONTOLOGY: The study of being; often used interchangeably with Metaphysics.

PANTHEISM: A world view that makes God identical with the world; "All is God and God is all." God is wholly Immanent, and therefore not transcendent.

PHENOMENA: In Kant, the world of appearance (how things appear to the senses); as opposed to the Noumena (world of reality). Also referred to as the phenomenal world.

PHILOSOPHY: Literally, the "love of wisdom"; an attempt to provide rational and coherent understanding of the fundamental questions of life.

PLATONISM: Of or pertaining to the philosophy of Plato (427-347 B.C.)

PLURALISM: The metaphysical view that ultimate reality consists of many things. Contrasted with Monism.

PRAGMATISM: An American philosophy which makes workability and practical consequences the test for truth.

RATIONALISM: Broadly speaking, the epistemological view that stresses reason as the test of truth. In a strict sense, the belief that at least some knowledge is acquired independent of sense experience. Contrasted with Empiricism.

REALISM: The metaphysical view that asserts that physical objects exist apart from being perceived; the belief that the essences of things possess objective reality.

RELATIVISM: The belief that no absolutes exist (in truth and/or ethics). Truth and morality vary from person to person, time to time, circumstance to circumstance.

SKEPTICISM: In a loose sense, to doubt, question, or suspend judgment on philosophical issues. In a strict sense, to deny that true knowledge is attainable.

SOCRATIC METHOD: Derived from the Greek philosopher Socrates, a method for finding truth and meaning through rigorous questioning.

SOLIPSISM: "I myself only exist." The only reality that exists is one's self.

SUBJECTIVE IDEALISM: The belief that things (ideas) are dependent upon perception for their particular existence.

SUBSTANCE: A thing's underlying essence; that which makes a thing what it is.

TABULA RASA: Literally, a "blank tablet". John Locke's empirical view that human beings possess no innate (inborn) ideas or principles.

TELEOLOGICAL ARGUMENT: A proof for the existence of God; design, beauty, harmony, and purposiveness in the universe require a cosmic architect (i.e., God). Known as the design argument, it was defended by Plato, but its most popular presentation was given by William Paley.

THEISM: The world view that affirms the existence of an infinite, personal God, who is the transcendent creator, and immanent sustainer of the world. Judaism, Christianity and Islam are examples of theistic religions.

THOMISM: Of or pertaining to the philosophical and theological though of St. Thomas Aquinas (1225-1274).

TRANSCENDENT: Beyond, or distinct from, the time/space world.

WELTANSCHAUUNG: German term, referring to a person's world view (a conceptual scheme for interpreting reality).

# Those Considered as Some of the Most Influential Philosophers of the "Modern Era"

1. Immanuel Kant
2. Martin Heidegger
3. Edmund Husserl
4. Isaac Newton
5. David Hume
6. Karl Popper
7. Soren Kierkegaard
8. Ludwig Wittgenstein
9. John Locke
10. Friedrich Nietzche
11. Jean-Paul Sartre
12. René Descartes
13. Karl Marx
14. Baruch Spinoza
15. Maurice Merleau-Ponty
16. Arthur Schopenhauer
17. G.W.F. Hegel
18. Charles Sanders Peirce
19. Thomas Hobbes
20. Jean Jacques Rousseau

# Some Famous Philosophical Quotes That Impact Modern Culture

"The unexamined life is not worth living"
> – Socrates

"The life of man (in a state of nature) is solitary, poor, nasty, brutish, and short"
> – Thomas Hobbes

"I think therefore I am" ("Cogito, ergo sum")
> – René Descartes

"What is rational is actual and what is actual is rational"
> – G. W. F. Hegel

"God is dead! He remains dead! And we have killed him."
> – Friedrich Nietzsche

"There is but one truly serious philosophical problem, and that is suicide"
> – Albert Camus

"To be is to be perceived" ("Esse est percipi")
> – Bishop George Berkeley

"Happiness is not an ideal of reason but of imagination"
> – Immanuel Kant

"Liberty consists in doing what one desires"
> – John Stuart Mill

"There is only one good, knowledge, and one evil, ignorance"
> – Socrates

"If God did not exist, it would be necessary to invent Him"
> – Voltaire

"We are what we repeatedly do. Excellence, then, is not an act, but a habit"
> – Aristotle

"Life must be understood backward. But it must be lived forward "
> – Soren Kierkegaard

"Is man merely a mistake of God's? Or God merely a mistake of man's?"
> – Friedrich Nietzsche

"I would never die for my beliefs because I might be wrong"
> – Bertrand Russell

"Religion is the sign of the oppressed ... it is the opium of the people"
> – Karl Marx

"Happiness is the highest good"
> – Aristotle

# SEAPC Career Link Trips

## Opportunities

### Cambodia

In conjunction with the Ministry of Education in Cambodia, you can teach English and all sports in the 488 public schools of Banteay Meanchey Province. There are 127,000 students in these schools from grade 1 through 12. The opportunities range from two weeks to two years and are accredited through an agreement with Geneva College in Beaver Falls, PA.

### Laos

In conjunction with the Ministry of Education of the Lao Peoples' Democratic Republic and Phon Tip University in Vientiane, Laos, the instructor can teach English, Math, Computer Science, Information Technology, and all Business courses.

### China

The South East Asia Prayer Center (SEAPC) has been invited by the Central Government of the People's Republic of China to develop protocols and practices concerning the treatment and education of children with Autism. Within this agreement, SEAPC has contracted with Cairn University in Langhorn, PA to receive the applications of interns, trainers and teachers to go to China on month-long teaching teams to work with children with Autism. Any student with a degree or seeking a degree in Education, Special Education, Speech Therapy, and Behavioral Science can be accepted to this program.

### Myanmar

In conjunction with the Ministry of Education and Acts Bible College in Yangon, there are opportunities to teach English, Computer Science, Information Technology and Math. The partnership between SEAPC and Acts Bible College provides an excellent platform for those wanting to build their career by adding intern experience in this rapidly emerging nation.

## How to Apply

Interested students should apply at www.SEAPC.org, via the SEAPC app, or by email to sarah@seapc.org.

Program costs, accrediting information and course content will be discussed with those who apply.

# National Campus Ministries

**Campus Outreach**
PO Box 43591
Birmingham, AL 35243
205-776-5516
www.campusoutreach.org

**CCO**
**(Coalition for Christian Outreach)**
5912 Penn Avenue
Pittsburgh, Pennsylvania 15206
412-363-3303
www.ccojubilee.org

**Chi Alpha Campus Ministries**
1445 N. Boonville Avenue
Springfield, MO 65802
417-862-2781 x1425
chialpha@ag.org
www.chialpha.com

**Cru**
100 Lake Hart Drive
Orlando, FL 32832
1-888-278-7233
www.cru.org

**Every Nation Campus Ministries**
everynation@everynation.org
www.everynation.org

**Fellowship of Christian Athletes**
8701 Leeds Road
Kansas City, MO 64129
800-289-0909
fca@fca.org
www.fca.org

**InterVarsity Christian Fellowship**
635 Science Drive
Madison, WI 53711-1099
608-274-9001
info@intervarsity.org
www.intervarsity.org

**The Navigators**
PO Box 6000
Colorado Springs, CO 80934
719-598-1212
info@navigators.org
www.navigators.org

**Reformed University Fellowship**
1700 N Brown Road, Suite 104
Lawrenceville, Georgia 30043
678-825-1070
info@ruf.org
www.ruf.org

**University Christian Outreach**
www.ucoweb.org

# About the Author

Mark Geppert responded to the call of God in July of 1973. At the Lord's direction he and his wife, Ellie, sold their thriving business and followed the Lord through Bible School and to the mission field. Sent by a local church to Guatemala in 1976, they began a life of mission that included evangelism, church planting, influence with government officials, and the miraculous.

The Lord used Mark to establish the Dayspring Bible Training Center, "Taking the Word to the World in the Eighties." From this center, teams went into many closed and limited access nations. By 1988, the Gepperts led hundreds of faith missionaries in restricted access areas. Mark became a Vice President of the Association of International Missions Services; networking the then 75,000 renewal churches to the then 17,000 unreached peoples.

The second meeting of the Lausanne Committee for World Evangelism in 1988 produced 7,000 papers on reaching the world with the gospel by the year 2000. Seeing the need for a prayer movement, Mark, Ellie and their sons, Sam and Matthew, moved to Singapore to begin walking in prayer the 10-40 window and the massive nation of Indonesia. Based in Singapore, they launched the South East Asia Prayer Center with the purpose of "Creating New and Networking Existing Prayer Cells." SEAPC has now grown into a very effective multinational ministry active in 75 countries.

The teaching heart of SEAPC is set forth in the book, *The Attack Lambs*. Now in its 10th English printing, this core teaching has become a part of the Chinese and North Indian church movements. It is translated into the languages of South East Asia and Chinese, Hindi, and Spanish.

Mark has written three other books, *BRIDGES*, *Stepping Stones*, and *Faith to Die For*. He travels the globe teaching prayer principles and mobilizing churches in prayer power. He can be contacted through www.seapc.org.

10-18

Thomas - Juana's dad

Glen

Miranda

Sally - Alabama

Barb - ~~brain~~ alzheimers

Barb - Colleen's mom   anger

Driving for Don

Juana

Gene Messick   Lauren
             niece's son

Mal 3:16